Singapore

D1457417

A Guide for Your Perfect
Singapore Adventure!

By: Project Nomad

Please Note

This is a travel book. Copyright © 2016 by Project Nomad. All rights reserved worldwide. No part of this publication may be reproduced or transmitted in any form without the prior written consent of the publisher. Limit of Liability/Disclaimer of Warranty: The publisher and author make no representations or warranties with respect to the accuracy or completeness of these contents and disclaim all warranties such as warranties of fitness for a particular purpose. The author or publisher is not liable for any damages whatsoever. The fact that an individual or organization is referred to in this document as a citation or source of information does not imply that the author or publisher endorses the information.

ISBN-13: 978-1541275072
ISBN-10: 1541275071

Contents

Introduction

Singapore, located at the southern peak of the Malaya Peninsula, is the island city-state. The city is spread over 60 islands, with the Singapore Island as its main island. After Monaco in the Mediterranean Sea, Singapore is the most densely populated area in the world, with around 5.5 million people living and working in the 718 km2 surface. Singapore is a prosperous and advanced city, commonly referred to as the Garden City. However, due to an extensive greening campaign, its swiftly became a City in a Garden.

Useful Information

Getting to Singapore

The International Changi Airport is the main international transportation hub of Singapore. It's also the easiest way to come to the city-state, if you don't travel from Peninsular Malaysia or certain destinations in Indonesia (Batam and Bintan). Besides the commercial airlines, low-cost plane companies use the Changi Airport too. Singapore is connected by direct flights to numerous destinations in Europe, the Americas, Asia, Australia and Africa.

Since the airport is located on the outskirts of the Main Island, transfer options are numerous and cheap. Transfers by the MRT (Mass Rapid Transit), trains and buses (from around S$2 upwards) are the cheapest options. Taxi's taxis (between S$20 and S$35, in general) tend to be more convenient for tourists with a lot of luggage. The Airport Shuttle service offers transfers to the passengers' hotels and hostels for S$9, excluding Sentosa Island. Passengers can rent a private shuttle for Sentosa Island for S$60. The airport shuttle operates 24/7, while taxis charge 50% higher fares between midnight and 6 a.m.

You can get to Singapore by bus from various destinations on the Malay Peninsula and from Bangkok Thailand. From Bangkok, it's over a full day of travel to Singapore by bus, and fares range between S$110 and S$130. From Kuala Lumpur Malaysia, fares are between S$25 and S$50, and travelling times are several hours.

Getting to Singapore by train takes up to 10 hours from Kuala Lumpur and up to 40 hours from Bangkok, and costs up to S$40 and S$100 respectively. If you don't mind splurging, take the Eastern & Oriental Express. It takes you on an amazing journey for a US$2700 price from Bangkok to Singapore.

You can also get to Singapore by boats and ferries from Indonesia and Malaysia, but travelling from Indonesia by boat tends to equal prices offered by airline companies. You can use ferries to access Singapore from Johor Bahru, in Malaysia. Singapore is also a popular port of call for various cruising companies.

Bonus knowledge: If you aren't laden with luggage, you can make substantial savings by flying to Johor Bahru instead to Singapore, and taking transfer from there.

Getting Around in Singapore

Getting around in Singapore is most efficient by trains of the MRT network, operating from 5:30 a.m. to midnight. Trains run every 5 to 7 minutes (up to 3 minutes at peak times), and most city attractions are a short walk away from the MRT stations. Single trip fares range between S$1.4 and S$2.5.

Singapore buses operate from 6 a.m. to midnight, and you can reach each corner of the city by the SBS Transit (buses) and SMRT (combining buses and metro) networks. Single trip tickets cost from S$1 to S$2.1. SMRT also runs several Night Rider (NR) services until 2 a.m., charging S$4.5 flat rate.

All Singaporean taxis operate on a meter (S$0.22 for every 400 meters + the S$3 flagfall), but finding a taxi is rather difficult at peak hours. A number of surcharges apply, such as the city-area surcharge from 5 p.m. to midnight (S$3), up to S$8 for telephone bookings, and more. Keep in mind that taxis aren't allowed to stop anywhere except at designated stands in the city center.

You can also explore the city by bike but be extra careful if you cycle on the roads because drivers tend to be aggressive. Use dedicated bike lanes where available and parks for cycling. The most affordable bike rentals are available on Pulau Ubin Island (around S$5/day), while bikes are rented for S$6/hour throughout the rest of Singapore.

From the Marina South Pier, you can set off onto various excursions to Singaporean islands by boat.

Bonus knowledge: if you are in Singapore a few days, you can benefit greatly of an EZ-Link Card (S$10/day, S$16/2-day, S$20/3-day cards) that offers unlimited rides on

Singapore buses and trains during the validity period.

Currency

The official currency in Singapore is the Singapore Dollar (S$ or SGD), which consists of 100 cents (S¢). Available banknote denominations are 1, 2, 5, 10, 20, 25, 50, 100, 500, 1000 and 10 000 S$, while coin denominations in use are 1, 5, 10, 20, 50 S¢ and S$1. Approximate exchange rates in regard to other major currencies are: 1 USD = 1.44 SGD; 1 EUR = 1.5 SGD; 1 GBP = 1.79 SGD; 1 AUD = 1.06 SGD.

ATMs are widely spread throughout Singapore and major credit cards are accepted in most shops and restaurants. Money exchange offices aren't hard to find either, but for the best rates you should check popular tourist hubs in the city, especially Mustafa Center in Little India, People's Park Complex in Chinatown and Parkway Parade in Marine Parade.

Tickets to major museums are between S$6 and S$15 and a midrange double room at a hotel costs between S$140 and S$250. Street vendor meals are up to S$5 and cocktails in bars are up to S$25.

Stay Safe

When it comes to safety in Singapore, you can relax while you explore. Night or day, the city-state is among the safest places on earth. Crime rates are extremely low thanks to rigorous punishments that are enforced on transgressors. All you have to do is use some common sense and keep your wallets and other belongings close, and you are highly unlikely to have troubles with theft.

However, what you should be aware of are local laws and may not be punishable from where you are from. If you spit on the street, you face a fine; the same holds true if you forget to flash a toilet. If you use another person's Wi-Fi, you risk a S$1000 fine, jail time or both. Smoking in public is also a bad idea. Therefore, carefully observe the Singaporean regulations before you come to this clean and well-regulated city.

Best Times to Visit Singapore

Due to its geographic position 150 kilometers north of the equator, Singapore has hot temperatures and high humidity throughout the year. Slightly cooler periods are from November to March. Temperature averages range between 24°C and 31°C (73°F and 88°F) most of the year, and the precipitation levels range between 150 mm (5.9 in) and 270 mm (10.6 in). July is the driest and December the wettest month. The lowest number of rainy days is February (13), while November and December have 25 rainy days on average. Average sea temperatures are at upper 20°C (over 80°F). Humidity levels range between 60% and 90% daily and are even higher during prolonged rainy periods.

Singapore is a year-round destination, without distinctive low and high seasons, although the summer's end and the beginning of the fall mark a slight break. Travel-related expenses are mostly uniform throughout the year.

Languages

Except elderly Singaporeans, everyone speaks English with various degrees of fluency in the city. English is one of the official languages in Singapore. Other official languages are Mandarin, Malay, Chinese and Tamil. Chinese is spoken by around 75% of the populace, Malay by 13% and Tamil (Indian) by 10%. Other major languages include Hindi and Punjabi.

Time Zone

Singapore is located in the Singapore Time zone (UTC+8). Compared to other major cities throughout the world, time in Singapore runs 3 hours behind Sydney Australia, 2:30 hours ahead of Delhi India, 7 hours ahead of Paris France and 13 hours ahead of New York in the U.S.A.

Electricity

The electricity runs at 230V in Singapore, and the British BS1363 three-pin socket is mostly used. If your appliances use different electricity (110V or 120V, like in the

U.S.A.), don't forget to bring the necessary adapters and converters with you.

A Short Historical Outline

Singapore was founded in the 14th century as the village of Tamasek, It was controlled by various kingdoms, empires and sultanates until the 19th century, when modern Singapore was established. In the 14th century, the settlement became an important port of the Kingdom of Singapura. By the end of the 14th century, it was overtaken by the Majapahit Empire. Mallaca and Johor Sultanates also used to be rulers of Singapore.

The British Empire established a trading post of the East India Company in 1819, and British public official Thomas Stamford Raffles, designed a plan for the urban development of the area. Singapore officially became a British Colony in 1824 by adjoining the Straits Settlements, a group of British controlled territories in the Malay Peninsula. It remained in colonial possession or under foreign rule until 1959. Back then, the population of Singapore didn't exceed 10 thousand.

Colonial rule was beneficial for Singapore. Due to the opening of the Suez Canal in Egypt, another British Colony, in 1869 and to the development of the steamships in the 1860s, Singapore became a significant port of call for vessels sailing between Asia and Europe. Its status as a free port increased the city's fast development.

In 1867, the British government took control over the prosperous city from the East India Company. By the 1870s, the population of Singapore had risen to 100 thousand people. Many grand city structures were built throughout the 19th and early 20th century including the Victoria Theatre & Concert Hall, Sri Srinivasa Perumal Temple and Leong San See Temple.

The Japanese bombing and occupation of the city during the Second World War, which lasted from February 1942 until August 1945, halted the continuous advancement of the city. With the return of the Brits, Singapore became a Crown Colony until 1959, when self-government was introduced. In 1963, the city joined with Malaysia, but the merging proved unsuccessful. Since 1965, Singapore has been recognized as an independent city-state with the steady economic growth.

Top attractions

Singapore is home to so many attractions that visiting them all is a challenge, even for the Singaporeans. These consist of gardens, parks, multicultural religious structures, museums and modern buildings. In the following section you can find some of the most popular Singaporean points of interest and landmarks.

1. Marina Bay

One of the most popular areas in Singapore, the Marina Bay boasts an engaging waterfront, striking architecture featuring futuristic designs, infinite shopping and entertaining opportunities, museums, parks and more. There are several walking trails in Marina Bay that should be explored to you can see the exuberant greenery, diverse wildlife consisting of migratory birds and monitor lizards and public art of the Garden City.

2. Marina Bay Sands

The Marina Bay Sands is among the most striking structures in the city, and could be considered a city of its own. Besides 2500 luxurious accommodation units, the structure houses a number of restaurants, theaters, up-scale stores, gardens and much more. The building is easily recognizable, consisting of three 55-story towers that are 200 meters tall and are topped by an observation deck called Sands SkyPark.

You don't need to be a guest to the Marina Bay Sands to pay it a visit. Besides engaging shopping throughout its endless halls, the structure's observation deck offers unparalleled views over the city. Make sure to bring your swimming suit. The pool, flanked by a lush garden with palm trees, is located just by the edge of the deck. Sunset is the best time for witnessing and appreciating the picturesque view over Singapore.

While you are in Singapore, spend some time in the evening hours at the waterfront, next to the Marina Bay Sands and ArtScience Museum. Wonderful musical performance that involves light shows, water and various visual effects are a must-see. The Wonder Full show lasts around 15 minutes and is the Southeast Asia's largest light and water show.

The observation deck of the Marina Bay Sands operates from 9:30 a.m. to 10 p.m. (11 p.m. on Friday and Saturday), and the full price admission fee is S$23.

Official website: https://www.marinabaysands.com/#stUvKH EQ1zhjdmgC.97

3. ArtScience Museum

The ArtScience Museum is another architecturally appealing structure in Marina Bay, featuring the shape of an open lotus flower. This ultra-modern museum is the exhibiting site of internationally acclaimed collections of art, and a venue that introduces contemporary works of art by local and Asian artists. In addition to noteworthy art pieces, the ArtScience Museum boasts a Rainwater waterfall, which is channeled through the center of the building from the roof.

Besides aforementioned temporary exhibitions, the museum stages permanent exhibitions underlining humankind's progress in arts and science throughout the ages.

The ArtScience Museum operates between 10 a.m. and 7 p.m

Ticket prices depend on the current exhibitions.

Official website:
http://www.marinabaysands.com/museum/about.html#FwlDugTOMbwEMiws.97

4. Waterfront Promenade

The 3.5-kilometer long stretch, which is part of the 11.7-kilometer route around the Marina Reservoir, is a beautiful promenade that introduces a couple of interesting points of interest along the Marina Bay. The promenade connects the Gardens by the Bay, Marina Barrage and Sports Hub, and some architecturally appealing landmarks.

The Helix Bridge, inspired by the structure of DNA, is one of the most unique bridges in the world. It is one of the must-see city landmarks, and is most magnificent at night when it's lit by thousands of LED lights. The bridge is a great spot for enjoying panoramic views of Singapore's skyline from its viewing platforms.

The Singapore Flyer, at the opposite side of the Marina Bay Sands, across the Helix Bridge, is one of the largest observation wheels in the world. The 158-meter tall structure probably offers the second best 360° views of Singapore (after the Marina Bay Sands' observation deck). For the most beautiful view, make sure to arrive at dusk.

If you come on a clear day, the views encompass parts of Malaysia and Indonesia.

Across the road from the Singapore Flyer, the Youth Olympic Park is the first art park in the city. It should be visited at both day and night, when the LED lights cast magical illumination and the majestic city lights define the Singapore's skyline.

The Esplanade Theatres, located farther away from the Helix Bridge, is another outstanding city landmark, featuring a shape of a Durian (a particular fruit). The venue is a favorite concert hall, theater and shopping mall.

Thanks to its nicely arranged areas, the Waterfront Promenade is the focal point for various public events, shows and performances.

5. Merlion Park

The Merlion Park, facing the Marina Bay Sands from the opposite side of the bay, is where the Singaporean national icon and its "cub" are located. Surely, you remember a strange being that features the body of a fish and the head of a lion from Singapore advertising campaigns? The body of the popular "Merlion" is in correlation with Singapore's history. The fish body symbolizes the city's beginnings as the fishing village Tamasek, meaning "sea town". The creature's head refers to the city's original name Singapora, meaning "lion city".

The larger Merlion is 8.6-meter tall, sprouting water from its mouth (take picture from the right angle for some extraordinary photos). Its cub, on the other hand, is "only" 2 meters tall. From the Merlion Park, you can take a bumboat (small water taxi) and explore marvelous structures along the Singapore River.

6. Gardens by the Bay

The Gardens by the Bay is a recent addition to Singapore's endless wonders. Boasting numerous first-class attractions, the 101-hectare property is divided into Bay South Garden, Bay East Garden and Bay Central Garden themed areas, next to the Marina Reservoir. The Gardens by the Bay is a multi-awarded horticultural establishment and one of the city's premium tourist attractions.

The complex's major attractions are Flower Dome and Cloud Forest conservatories and supertrees. There are 18 supertrees throughout the complex, with the Supertree Grove alone having 12 of them. The Grove's supertrees range between 25 and 50 meters in height, housing hundreds of plant and flower species that make them vertical gardens. Ferns, orchids (Singapore's national flower) and bromeliads are to found, among other species. Tops of supertrees, radiating in different directions from the trunk, provide shade during the day and become a resplendent sight at night, illuminated by numerous sparkling hues of the light display.

The best spot for observing the Gardens by the Bay from a bird's eye view is the Supertree-top Bistro, located atop the tallest supertree. Also, don't miss the OCBC Skyway, a 128-meter long walkway for engaging aerial views of the gardens.

The Flower Dome, which is "only" 38 meters tall, is recognizable by its incredible design. What is kept inside will impress you more. The Flower Dome is an exhibition space of plant species native to various regions of the world, with a Spanish olive tree that is around a millennium old. The facility consists of 7 themed zones, with each of them housing plants from different geographical regions like Africa, Australia and South America.

The Cloud Forest allows you to take a walk among the clouds and around a 35-meter tall mountain. The climate within this unique facility is set to feature conditions that reign between a 1000 and 2000-meter height above the sea level. The display encompasses various plants that prosper at that height in Central and South America and Southeast Asia. Among other species, you can see ferns, orchids, bromeliads and clubmosses – the representatives of one of the most ancient land plants. Atop the Cloud Forest, take a look at carnivorous plants in the Lost World section, and experience magnificent views of the Marina Bay waterfront. On your way down, various stalactites and stalagmites are introduced in the Crystal Mountain zone. The Cloud Forest also boasts the 35-meter tall indoor waterfall.

Other attractions of the Gardens by the Bay shouldn't be left unexplored. Throughout the complex, you can relax while on a pleasant walk along the promenades, take a look at diverse themed gardens, or let your children play in the Children's Garden on the trampolines, hanging bridges and the adventure playground. You'll also appreciate Chinese, Malay, Indian and English Heritage gardens if you have the time to see them. For a quick visit, make use of the Gardens' minibus.

Operating hours of the Gardens' points of interest vary, as well as admission fees. You can check the official website for details.

Official website:
http://www.gardensbythebay.com.sg/en.html

7. Buddha Tooth Relic Temple and Museum

A short walk to the southwest of Merilion Park will take you to the Chinatown district, where some surprising attractions are located. You will probably find the Thian Hock King Temple first. The temple is the oldest Buddhist temple in Singapore, featuring traditional southern Chinese architectural style. The temple was entirely built without the use of nails. Its amazing decoration comprises of statues and carvings of dragons, deities and phoenixes. The oldest Hindu temple in the city is located nearby. The Sri Mariamman Temple is a National Monument, whose tiered façade abounds with figures of deities and mythological beings.

The Buddha Tooth Relic Temple and Museum, however, is Chinatown's top attraction. Sheltering the supposed tooth relic of Buddha, the temple is an important cultural institution. Here, you can learn about the Buddhist religion. The BTRTM is the present century's addition, built to shelter the tooth relic that was uncovered from the collapsed stupa (a Buddhist structure that shelters relics) in Myanmar.

The BTRTM is the 4-storey Tang Dynasty-styled structure, displaying various artifacts that introduce visitors to Buddhism. The decoration of the temple consists of the Naga creatures (half human, half snake beings) and dragon carvings (dragons symbolize strength, luck and good fortune) among other sculptures. All the details flawlessly fit into a harmonious unity.

The temple has a couple of exhibition halls, a theatre and a contemplation hall among other facilities (a tearoom, library, courtyard…). The Buddhist Culture Museum on the 3rd level, and the Sacred Light Temple on the 4th level, are the temple's most significant facilities. The former exhibits the Buddhist artifacts, promoting the Buddhist religion's art and culture; the latter shelters the holy tooth relic. Besides the stupa containing the relic, the Sacred Light Temple boasts extraordinary details, consisting of dozens dragon carvings, Heavenly Devas (supernatural beings with various powers) and Confession Buddhas.

The BTRTM is open daily from 7 a.m. to 7 p.m. and the admission is free.

Website: http://www.btrts.org.sg/

Bonus knowledge: Naga creatures are guardians of the Buddhist temples and relics. Nagas can completely assume either human or snake forms.

Once the Buddha tooth relic was displayed, a controversy arose whether it truly belonged to Buddha. Some dental specialists even stated that the tooth isn't of human origins.

8. Little India

Little India is a vibrant district to the north of Marina Bay, with numerous shopping opportunities. It also boasts the number of Buddhist, Hindu and Muslim religious structures. Since Little India is rather a small district and has the highest number of such structures per-capita in Singapore, all of its attractions can be toured in a couple of hours. Sri Veeramakaliamman and Sri Srinivasa Perumal temples are the district's highlights.

9. Sri Veeramakaliamman Temple

The temple whose name is hard to pronounce, is devoted to the fierce Hindu deity Kali, who is represented by standing on her husband's corpse and wearing a necklace of human heads. Despite being displayed in such a manner, Kali is the protector of good people and mother of Ganesh, one of the most revered Hindu deities.

The temple's exquisite artwork includes figures of various Hindu deities adorning its façade and interior. Among other Hindu deities, you can learn about Ganesh the patron of art, Durga the goddess of victory and wealth, and Ramar, a version of Rama, a popular Ramayana epic hero and god.

The Sri Veeramakaliamman Temple operates daily (8 a.m. – 12:30 p.m.; 2 p.m. – 8:30 p.m.) and the entry is free.

Website:
http://www.sriveeramakaliamman.com/

10. Sri Srinivasa Perumal Temple

The Perumal Temple is another National Monument of Singapore and is the city's largest temple. The temple is devoted to Vishnu (Perumal), a multiple times reincarnated Hindu deity who is the embodiment of mercy and kindness. The temple's imposing pyramid-shaped Gopuram (tower) is elaborately decorated and visible from far away.

You may see a myriad of different statues adorning the Gopuram, but all of them are representations of Vishnu through his various reincarnations. Once inside, you'll get acquainted with other major Hindu deities. Lakshmi is Vishnu's consort, an embodiment of beauty and the goddess of love and Andal, Vishnu's 2nd consort, is an Alvar saint (12 Alvars are poet-saints devoted to Vishnu). Also, note Garuda, the mythical flying beast that is Vishnu's mount; Garudas are natural opponents to Nagas.

The temple is also home to extraordinary paintings and works of art including a beautifully decorated ceiling depicting 9 planets of the universe. The Sri Srinivasa Perumal Temple's courtyard is also a place of worship.

The temple's operating hours vary, and the admission is free. Check the official website for the details.

Website: http://www.sspt.org.sg/

Bonus knowledge: Vishnu forms the holy trinity of the Hinduism with Brahma, the creator, and Shiva, the destroyer. Vishnu is also known as Krishna, who is one of his reincarnations.

The immense height of the temple allows people who are unable to come for prayer, to worship from a distance.

11. National Museum of Singapore

A comprehensive display of Singapore's turbulent history is represented in the city's National Museum, which is another National Monument. Beautifully designed, the museum boasts Neo-Palladian and Renaissance styles, and is dominated by a dome. Singapore's history is displayed through numerous artifacts and multimedia presentations.

The National Museum has an innovative way of leading people through the city's engaging history by means of storytelling. If you would enjoy a comprehensive view of the city's eventful history, take the Events Path. The Personal Path allows you to witness changes from the common person's perspective. Among countless exhibits, of special significance are 10 designated National Treasures. Make sure to take a look at the *Singapore Stone, Mace of Singapore* and *Swettenham's Portrait* among other exhibits. In addition to the priceless historical value, these exhibits point out how Singapore developed into a stable multi-ethnic and multi-religious community.

The National Museum of Singapore operates daily from 10 a.m. until 7 p.m. The full price admission is S$15.

Website: http://nationalmuseum.sg/

12. Singapore Botanic Gardens

One of the main reasons why Singapore was named "the Garden City" is the Singapore Botanic Gardens. Besides marveling at the diversity of floral and herbal species, you can go jogging, picnicking and of other favorite leisure activities in this heaven of nature in the midst of the bustling city.

Consisting of various sections and sub-sections, the Gardens cover a 74-acre property and the UNESCO World Heritage Site. The Singapore Botanic Gardens feature endlessly charming and beautifully landscaped areas, with a number of them that could be pointed out as highlights. If your time is limited, make sure to see the National Orchid Garden, Bonsai Garden and Swan Lake.

The Orchid Garden boasts a stunningly varied collection of orchids, encompassing a few thousand species and hybrids. The garden is the largest orchid display in the world. Bonsai crafting and tree-shaping techniques are displayed in the homonymous garden, applied on dozens of tropical and sub-tropical specimens.

Introduced by the *Flight of Swans* sculpture, the Swan Lake area is a display of diverse aquatic plants and fish species. One of this site's curiosities is related to the 1890's, when a crocodile tried to make it its home.

The Singapore Botanic Gardens' complex is open daily from 5 a.m. until midnight and the admission is free, with the exception of selected sites.

Website: https://www.sbg.org.sg/

13. Singapore Zoo

The Singapore Zoo is without a doubt one of the best zoos in the world and among the city's top attractions. Animals freely roam in the enclosures featuring their natural habitat and some zoo's sections are organized as meeting points where people can interact with the wildlife. There are 11 themed zones within the complex, including the Frozen Tundra, Wild Africa, Australian Outback and Reptile Garden.

The Singapore Zoo is renowned for having the world's largest colony of orangutans. The zoo is spread out over a 28-hectare area, and if you are a first-time visitor, you should take a guided tram ride for the initial exploration. Special shows take place daily, and visitors are allowed to participate in some of them. Among everything else, you can see a playing dead performance by elephants, share your meal with orangutans and be entertained by sea lion performances.

The zoo is open daily from 8:30 a.m. to 6 p.m. and the full price fee is S$33.

Website: http://www.zoo.com.sg/

14. Sentosa Island

One of the most visited places in Singapore is Sentosa Island, located at the southern tip of the city-state. The island is a popular recreational area, with abundant vegetation, marvelous beaches, a number of entertaining and leisure facilities and hotels.

The majority of the island's surface is covered by the rainforest, while the beaches feature coconut palms. The Sentosa Island has a number of points of interest, with the Fort Siloso, Underwater World and Dolphin Lagoon and Tiger Sky Tower as some of the premium attractions.

The Fort Siloso used to be a defensive structure that controlled the entrance into Singapore. The fort was built by the Brits in the 1880s and is still equipped with the canons deployed before the Japanese aggression. However, the canons were pointed the wrong way; the Japanese arrived from the Malay Peninsula's direction.

The Underwater World is an entertaining and educational facility, where you can observe diverse sea and fresh water wildlife, and even dive among the sharks and dolphins.

The 110-meter tall Tiger Sky Tower is the tallest freestanding observation platform in Asia, offering views over Sentosa Island, Singapore and parts of Malaysia on a clear day.

Bonus knowledge: on Sentosa Island you can examine the huge 37-meter tall Merlion sculpture.

Additional Major Points of Interest

Singapore has a large number of extraordinary landmarks and tourist points of interest. Aside of the aforementioned, you should also visit the following if your schedule allows.

❖ **Masjid Sultan Mosque** is the most significant of Singapore's 80 mosques, and one of the most architecturally appealing structures in the city. The mosque is a combination of the Saracenic style and Indian elements.

❖ **Asian Civilizations Museum** introduces Asian cultures and those that are closely related to Singapore. A wide range of exhibits includes porcelain figures, textiles, precious metal items and calligraphy among others.

❖ **Fort Canning** in the park used to be the main defensive facility of Singapore, built by the Brits in 1859. Nowadays, various concerts, festivals, theatrical performances and art events take place in the fort and in the surrounding gardens.

❖ **Raffles Hotel** is tightly connected to the city's origins. The grand 19th century structure is in the vicinity of the site where Sir Stamford Raffles landed in Singapore. The marvelous building is set in a veritable oasis.

❖ **Bukit Timah Nature Reserve** is Singapore's highest hill, inhabited by diverse wildlife and plant species.

❖ **Maha Sasana Ramsi** is the Burmese Buddhist Temple, housing the largest white marble Buddha statue outside of Myanmar.

Singapore Shopping

Shopping is an important part of the Singaporean experience, and some best places in the city are:

❖ **Orchard Road's** shopping capacity is unbeatable. This stretch of land is home to more than 20 shopping malls and is overwhelmed with designer stores and shops frequented by bargain hunters. For the upscale shopping, head to ION Orchard and Paragon, while cheaper shopping can be found in Far East Asia and Lucky Plaza shopping centers.

❖ **Vivo City**, facing Sentosa Island, is the largest shopping mall in the city. Vivo City is described as a place where you can find everything including jewelry, Swiss watches, clothing, books, footwear, groceries, and so on. The shopping center includes entertaining and leisure facilities, wellness centers, spas and cinemas. In short, the term "city" describes this fascinating shopping mall completely.

❖ **Chinatown Street Market** is another unavoidable part of the Singaporean shopping experience, where countless stalls sell everything imaginable, from candles to artwork. While looking around, sample delicious and affordable street food.

❖ **Little India's Serangoon Road** is another destination for bargain hunters, whether you are looking for electronic appliances, Indian fabrics, garments or something else.

Singapore Leisure Activities

With endless sightseeing and shopping opportunities, allocating some time for leisure activities tends to be a bit difficult in Singapore. But if you manage, consider the potential activities a good investment of your time.

❖ Take a walk along the **picturesque Clarke Quai** and enjoy exquisite dining in its waterfront restaurants.

❖ Take a cruise along the **Singapore River** either by day or night, and be amazed by the city's expanse and romantic evening vibe. You can choose between bumboats and cruisers, which take off from the Clarke Quai, and appreciate various landmarks of this engaging metropolis – the Cavenagh Bridge, Parliament House, Raffle's statue, where the statesman reportedly first landed in Singapore, and many others. Evening cruises are especially romantic, with the Chinese lanterns lit and the city lights in the background.

❖ Take a **Singapore Cable** Car ride, operating between Mount Faber to Sentosa Island, for additional spectacular views over the "Lion City". If you like the experience, you can arrange a romantic dinner onboard the cable car.

Where to stay in Singapore

Finding good accommodations in Singapore is simple, and the following hotels are recommended

❖ The 4-star **York Hotel** is a convenient choice for passionate shopaholics as Orchard Road is nearby, and so is Marina Bay, Little India and Singapore Botanic Gardens. The hotel offers affordable prices for its premium location. York Hotel's rooms are sizable and comfortable, while the staff is professional and friendly. The hotel is especially convenient for families with children.

❖ In the 5-star **Marina Bay Sands** you get everything including 24-hour room service, the highest and longest swimming pool on the roof in the world and shopping and leisure opportunities within walking distance. The views of the city are unparalleled through floor-to-ceiling windows in the rooms.

❖ **My highest recommendation** is to use Airbnb where one can get a great apartment at different budgets that best fit your needs. Many times, one can get amazing deals and can save a lot of money, time and effort and live in an extraordinarily nice apartment in a great location. Also, many Airbnb hosts can pick you up from the airport and give you insider tips on the city from a truly local perspective. Best of all some Airbnb hosts can become live long friends! Here is a link courtesy of Project Nomad for $35 off your first trip to Bolivia or anywhere else you want to visit http://bit.ly/airbnbprojectnomad

61555551R00031

Made in the USA
Lexington, KY
14 March 2017